hello

© Copyright 2021-2025 - All rights reserved.

You may not reproduce, duplicate or send the contents of this book without direct written permission from the author. You cannot hereby despite any circumstance blame the publisher or hold him or her to legal responsibility for any reparation, compensations, or monetary forfeiture owing to the information included herein, either in a direct or an indirect way.

Legal Notice: This book has copyright protection. You can use the book for personal purpose. You should not sell, use, alter, distribute, quote, take excerpts or paraphrase in part or whole the material contained in this book without obtaining the permission of the author first.

Disclaimer Notice: You must take note that the information in this document is for casual reading and entertainment purposes only. We have made every attempt to provide accurate, up to date and reliable information. We do not express or imply guarantees of any kind. The persons who read admit that the writer is not occupied in giving legal, financial, medical or other advice. We put this book content by sourcing various places.

Please consult a licensed professional before you try any techniques shown in this book. By going through this document, the book lover comes to an agreement that under no situation is the author accountable for any forfeiture, direct or indirect, which they may incur because of the use of material contained in this document, including, but not limited to, —errors, omissions, or inaccuracies.

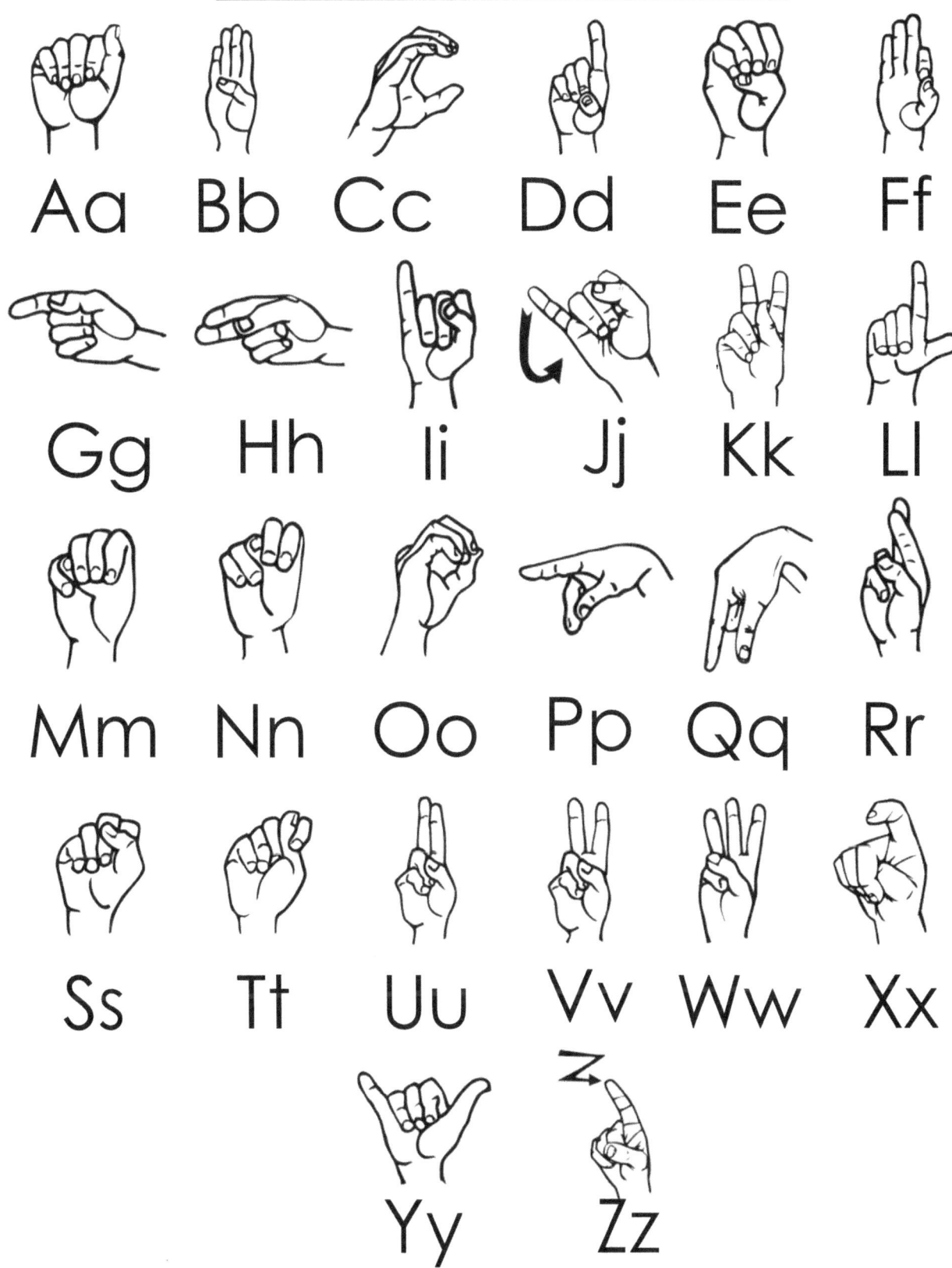

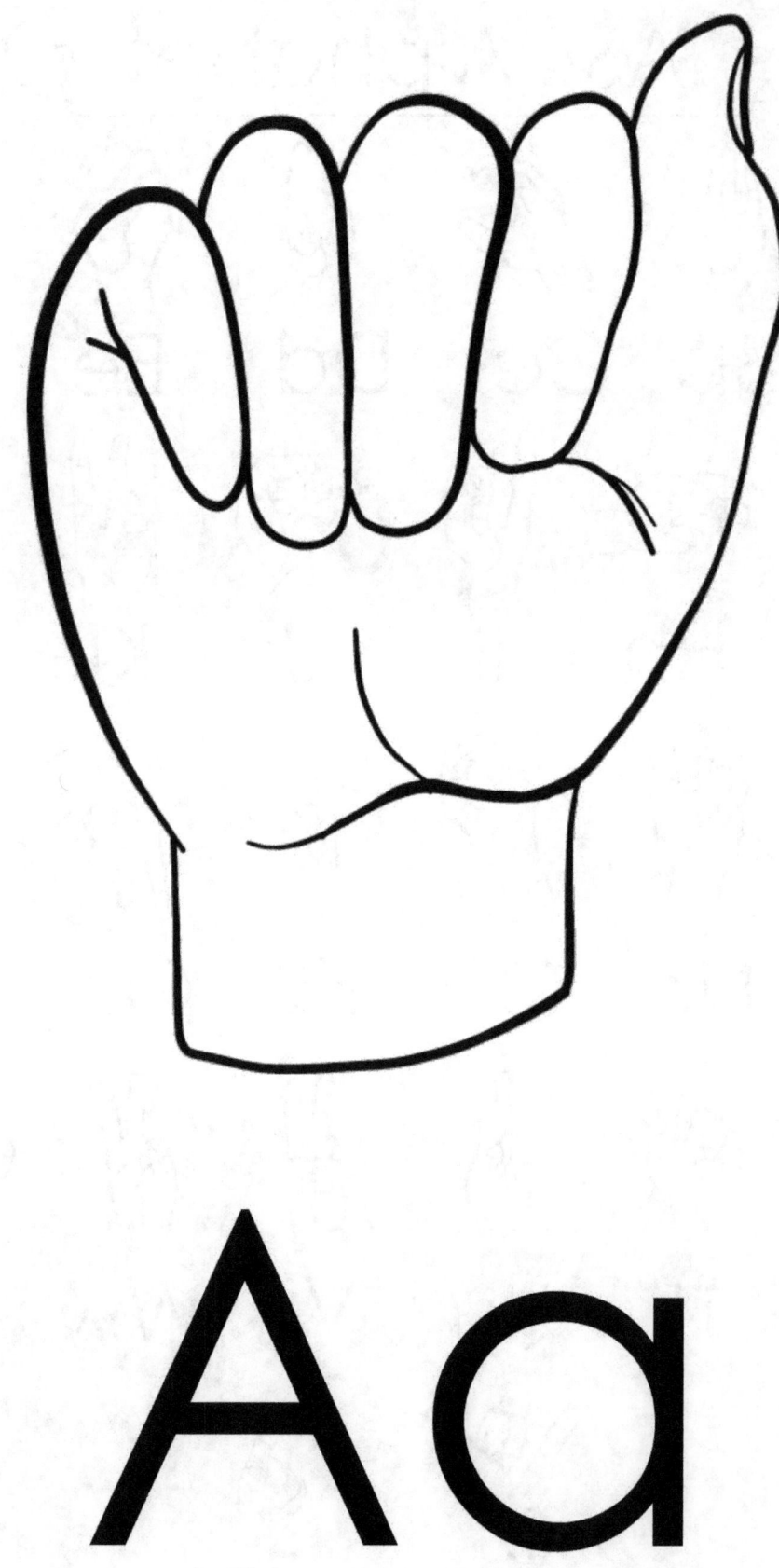

Aa

Trace and Sign the Alphabet

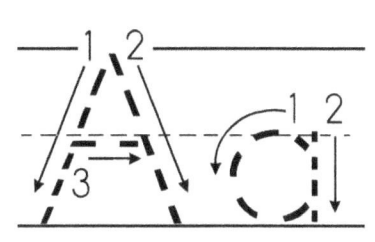 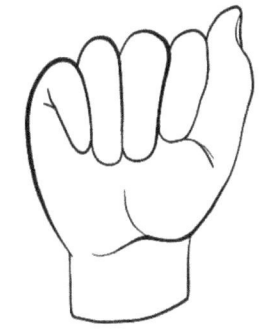

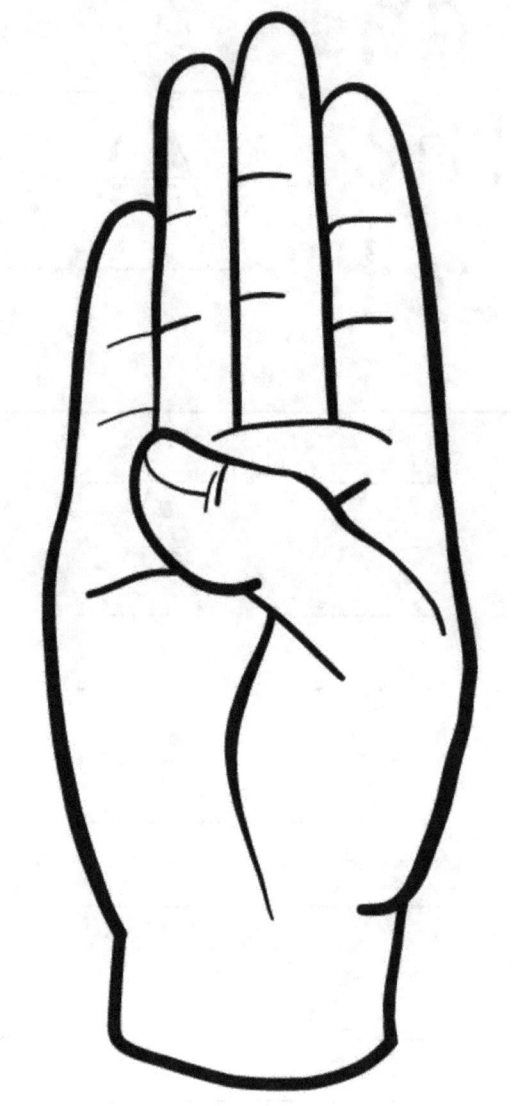

Bb

Trace and Sign the Alphabet

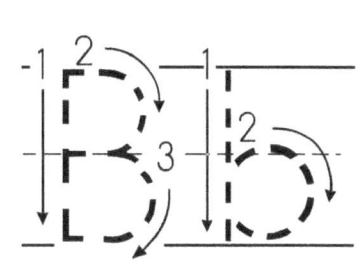
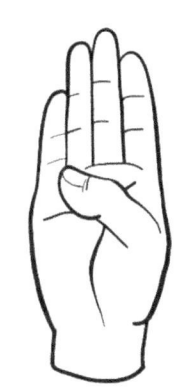

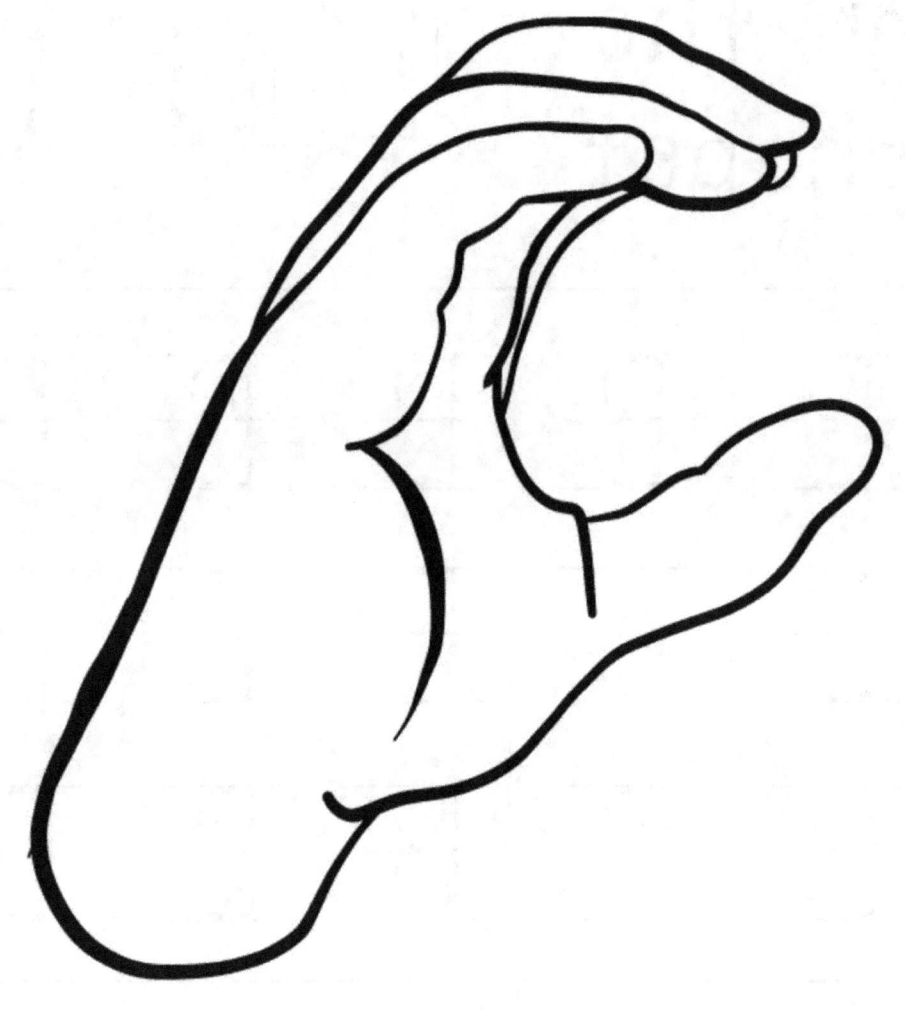

Cc

Trace and Sign the Alphabet

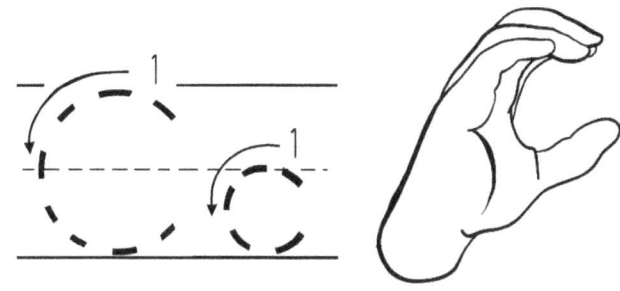

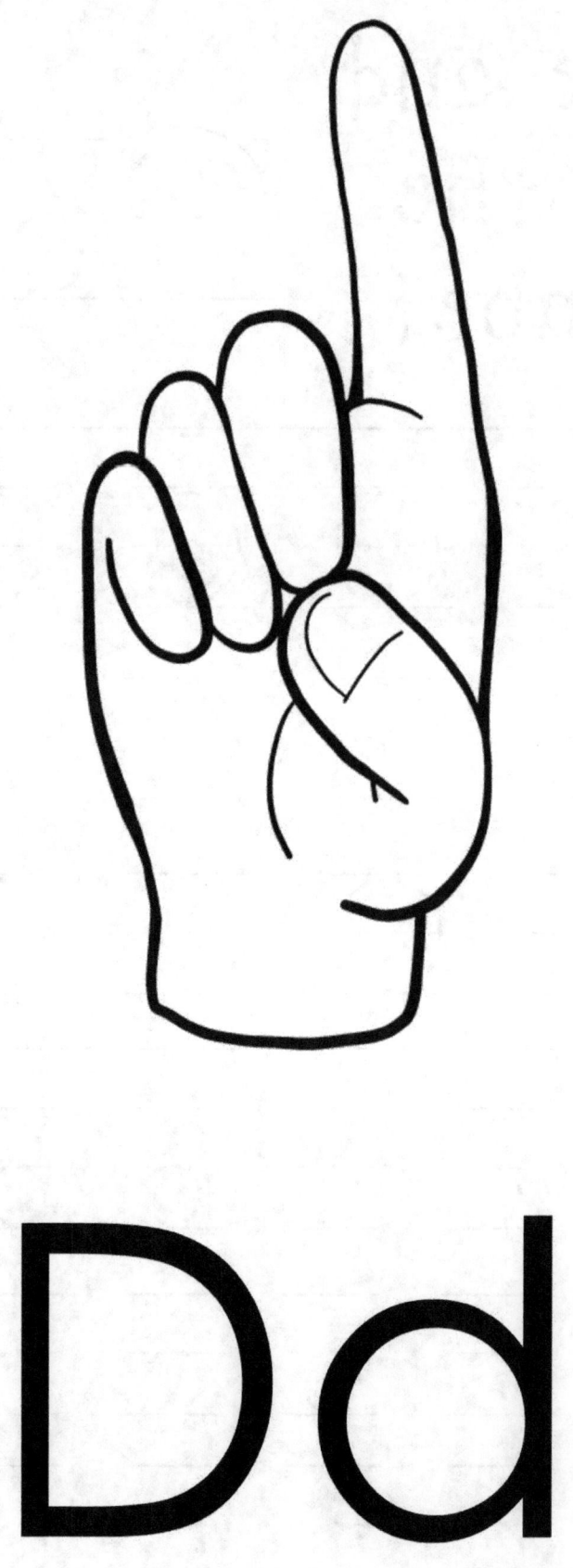

Dd

Trace and Sign the Alphabet

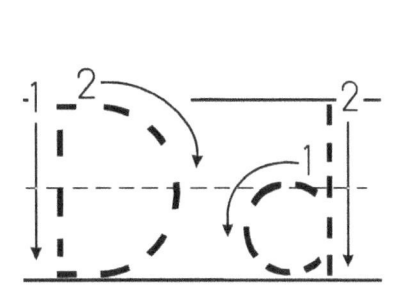 

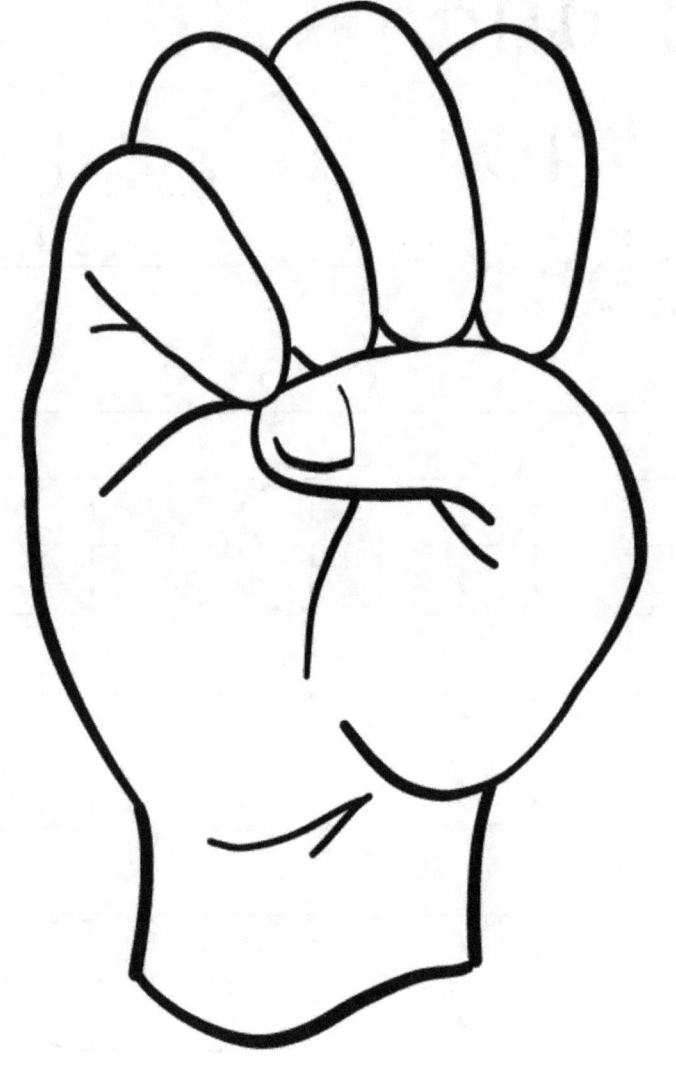

Ee

Trace and Sign the Alphabet

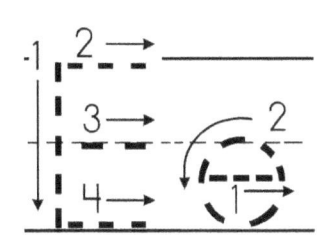

E E E E E E
E E E E E E
E E E E E E

e e e e e e
e e e e e e
e e e e e e

Ff

Trace and Sign the Alphabet

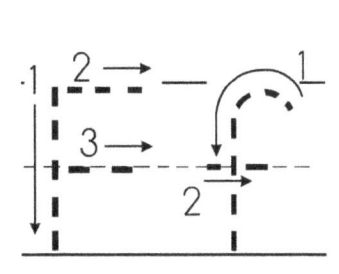
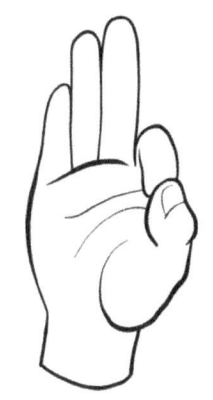

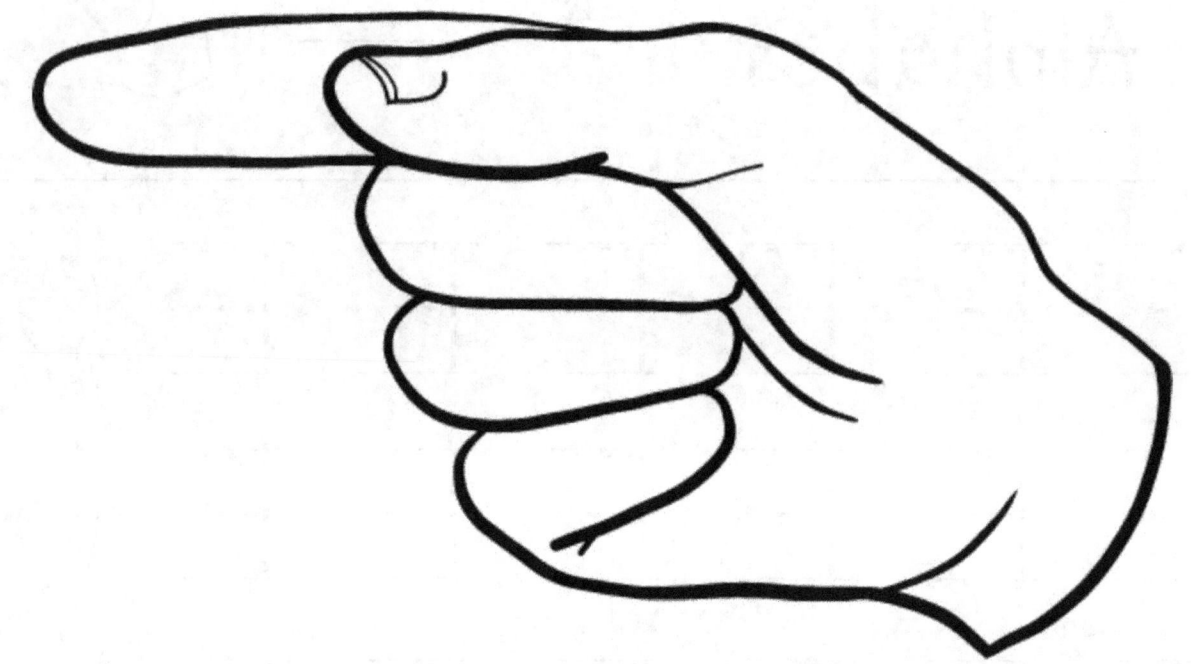

Gg

Trace and Sign the Alphabet

G G G G G

G G G G G

G G G G G

g g g g g g

g g g g g g

g g g g g g

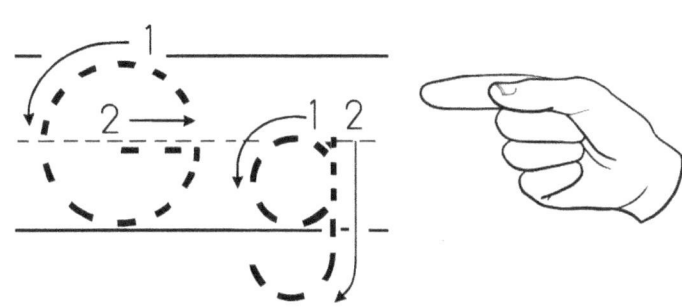

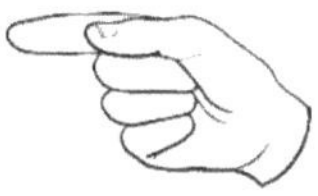

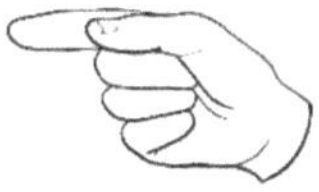

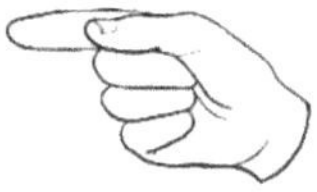

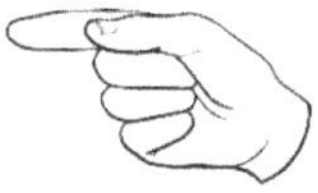

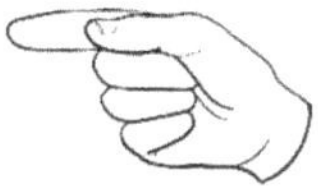

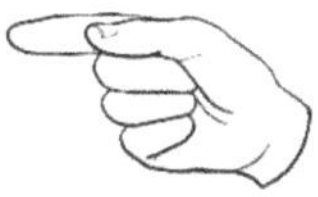

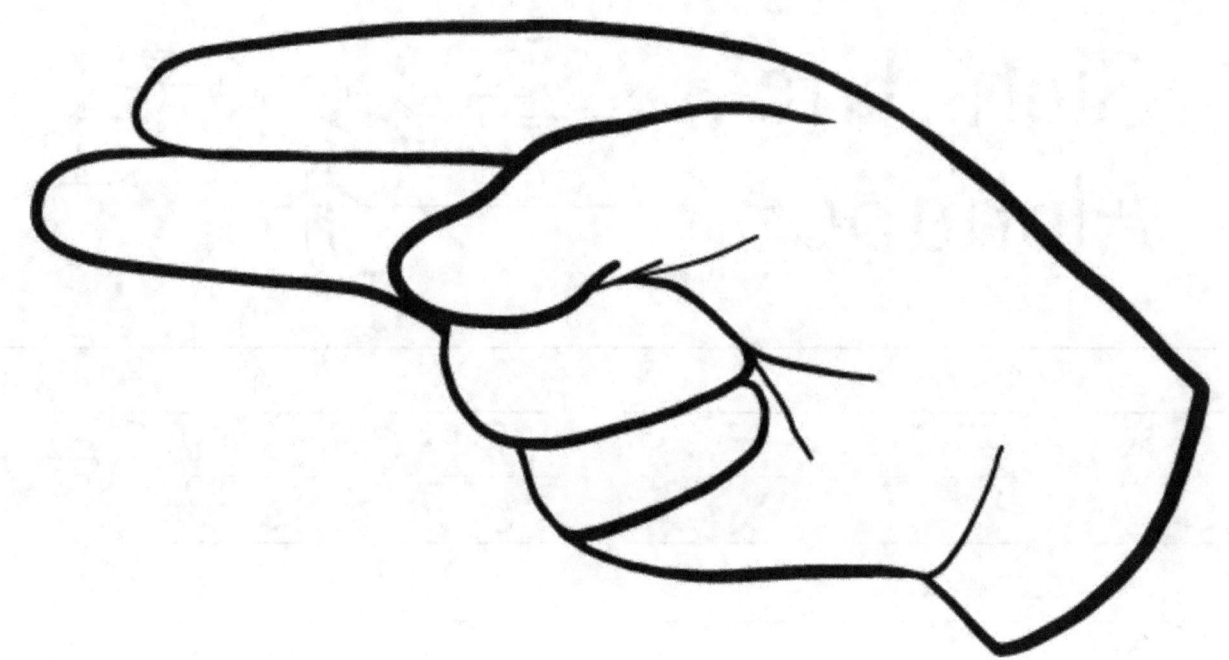

Hh

Trace and Sign the Alphabet

H H H H H

H H H H H

H H H H H

h h h h h h

h h h h h h

h h h h h h

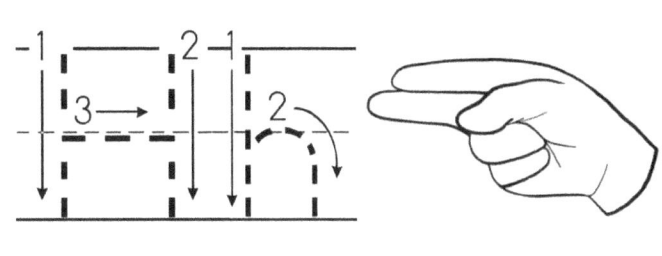

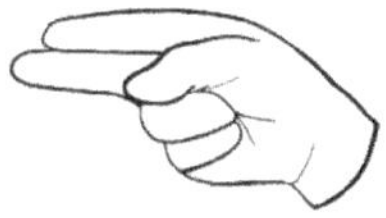

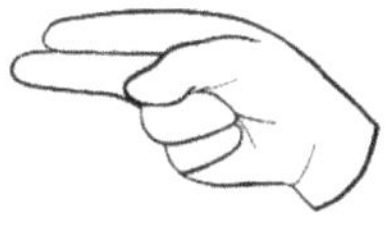

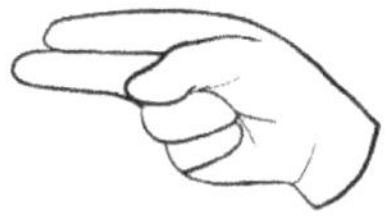

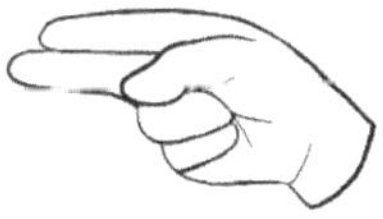

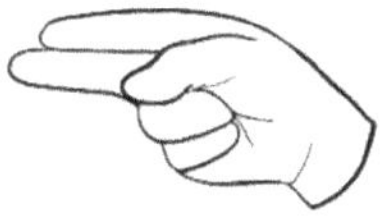

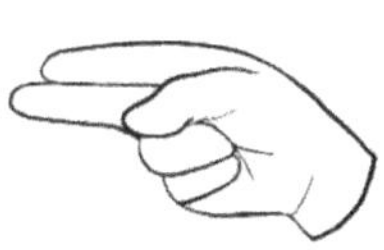

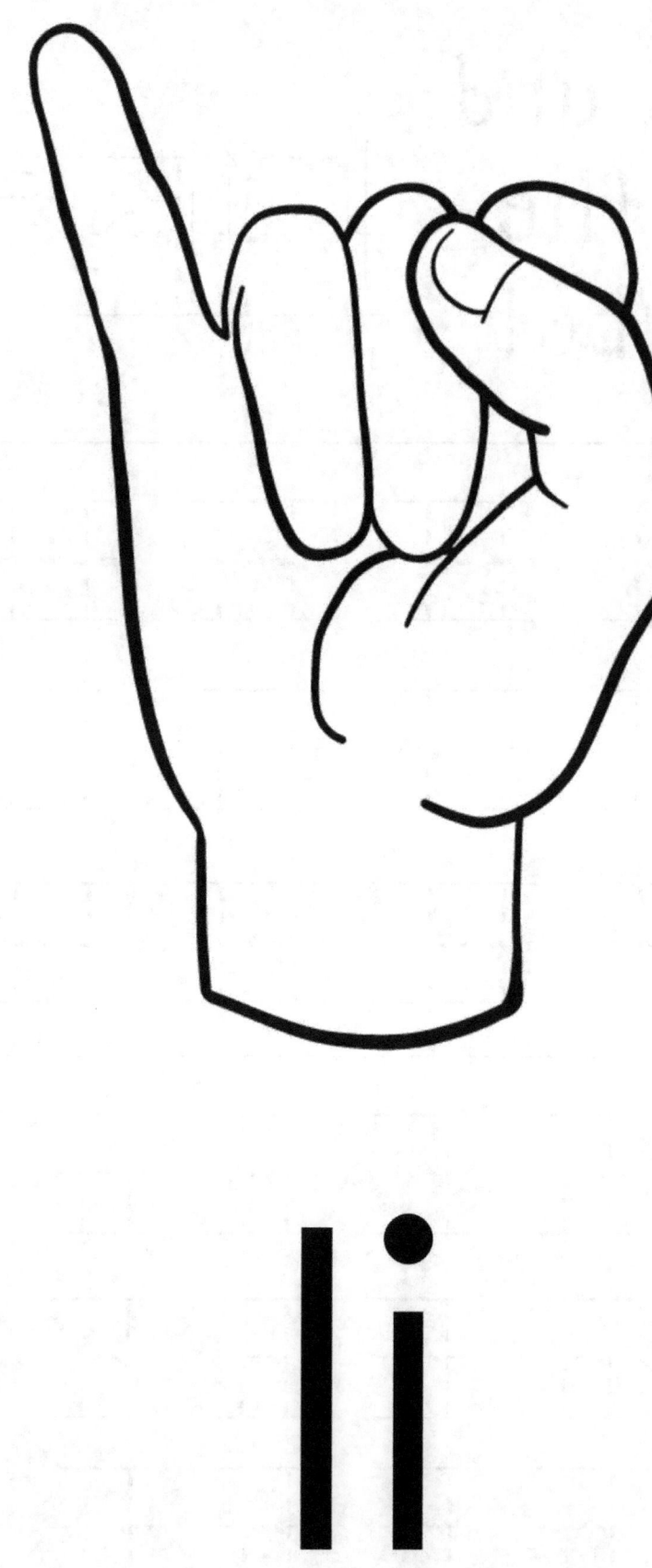

Ii

Trace and Sign the Alphabet

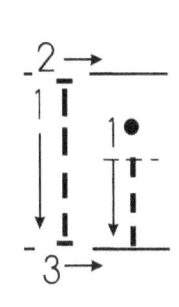

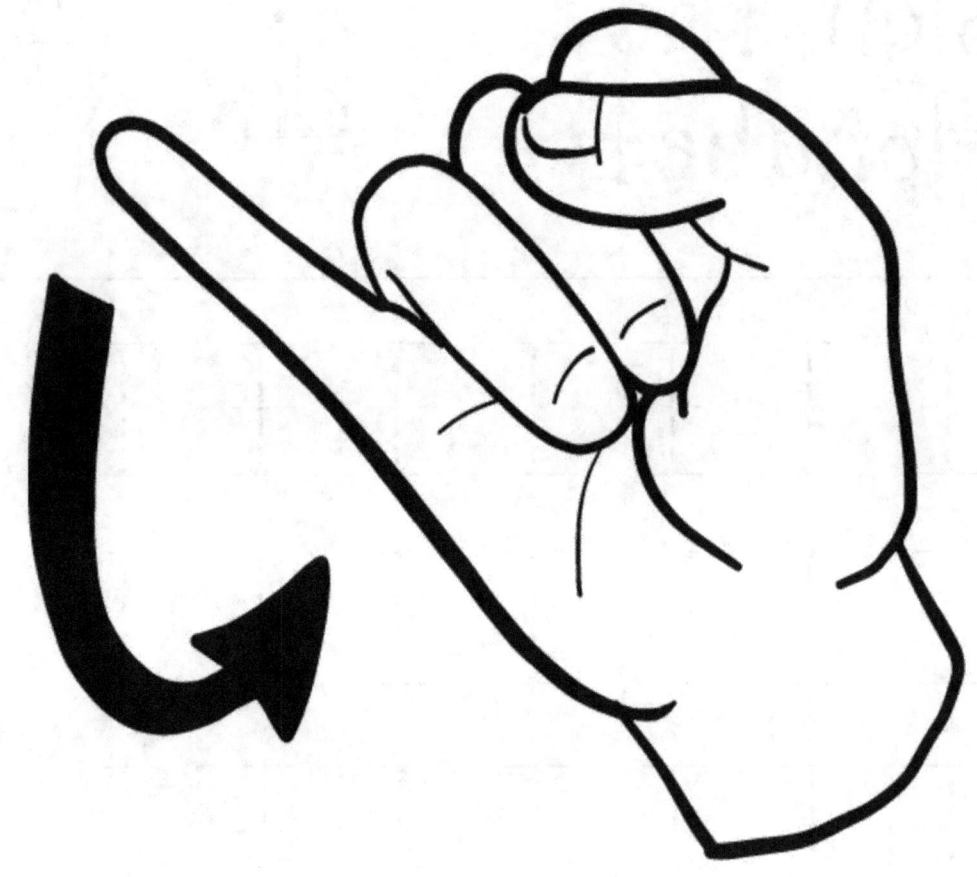

Jj

Trace and Sign the Alphabet

J j

J J J J J J

J J J J J J

J J J J J J

j j j j j j j j

j j j j j j j j

j j j j j j j j

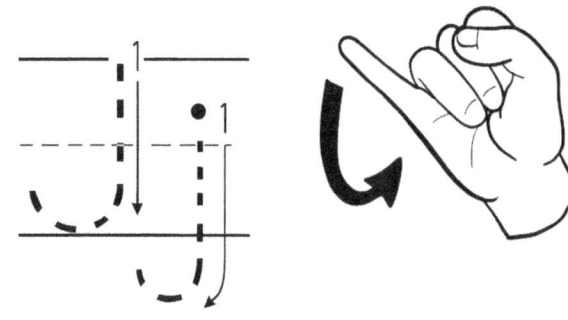

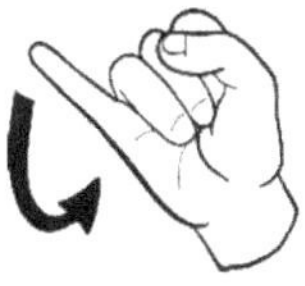

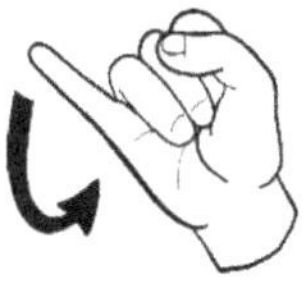

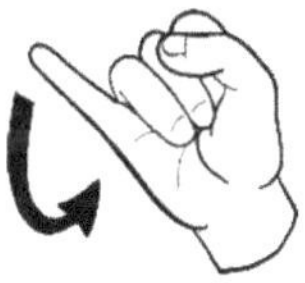

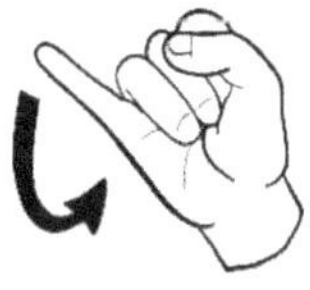

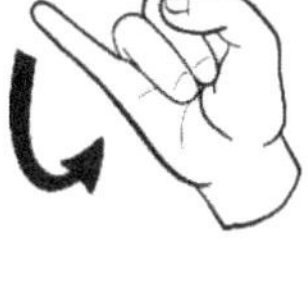

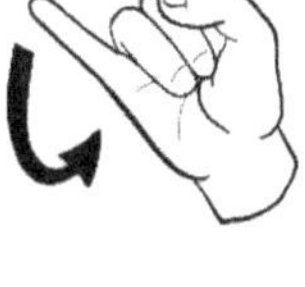

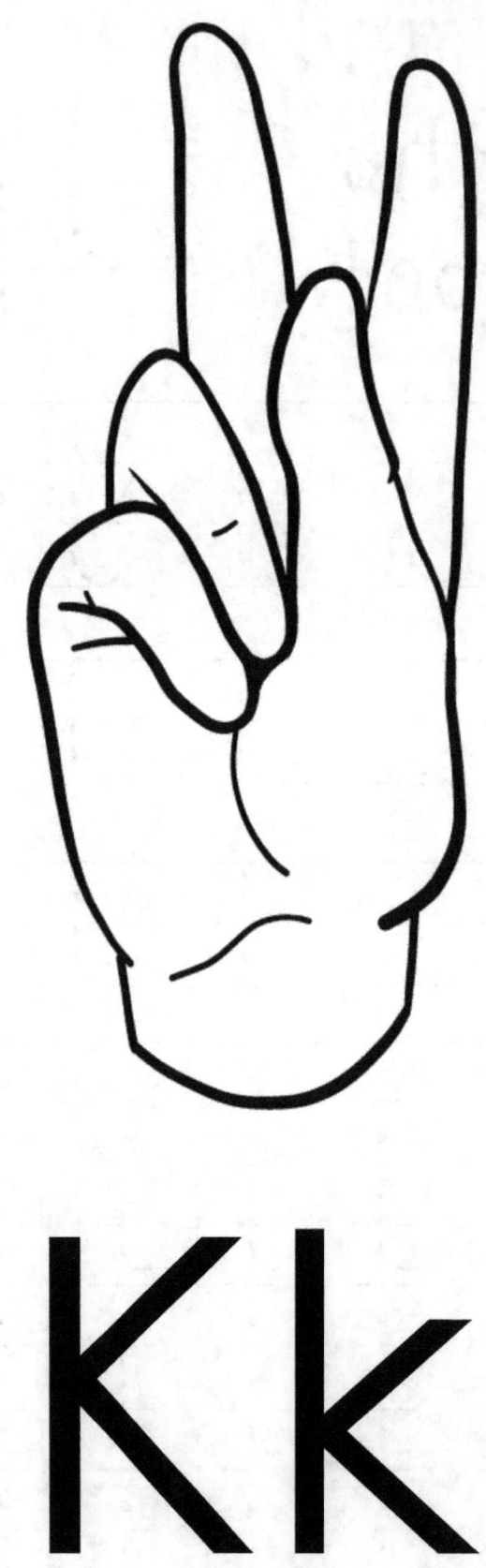

Kk

Trace and Sign the Alphabet

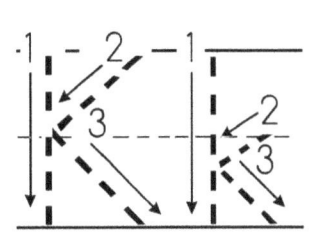 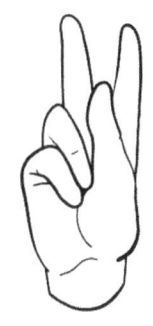

K K K K K K

K K K K K K

K K K K K K

k k k k k k

k k k k k k

k k k k k k

Ll

Trace and Sign the Alphabet

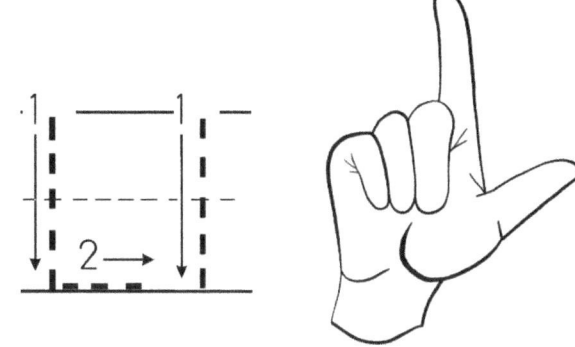

Mm

Trace and Sign the Alphabet

M M M M

M M M M

M M M M

m m m m m

m m m m m

m m m m m

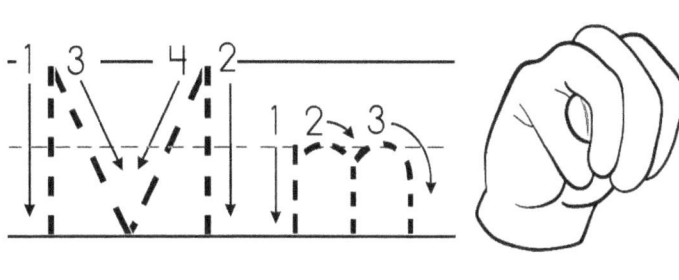

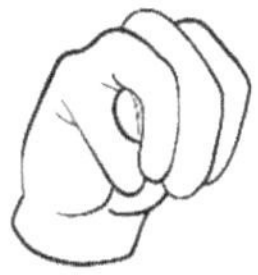

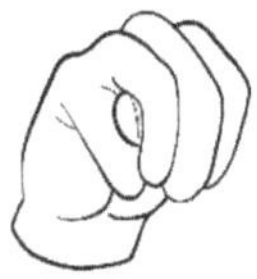

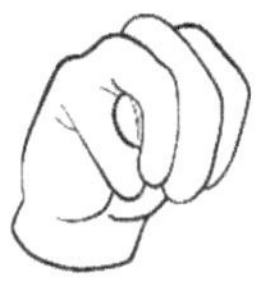

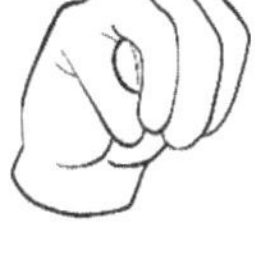

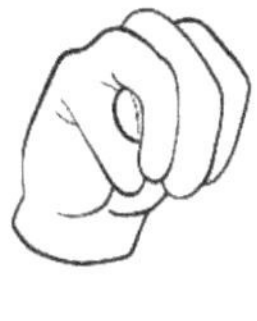

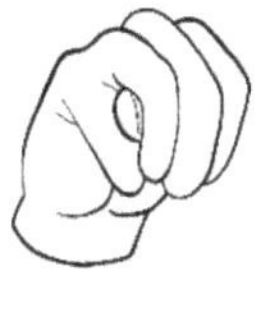

Nn

Trace and Sign the Alphabet

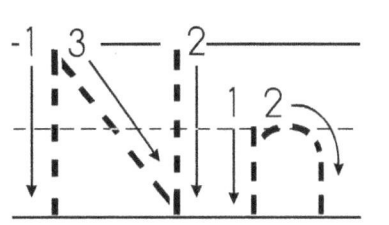 

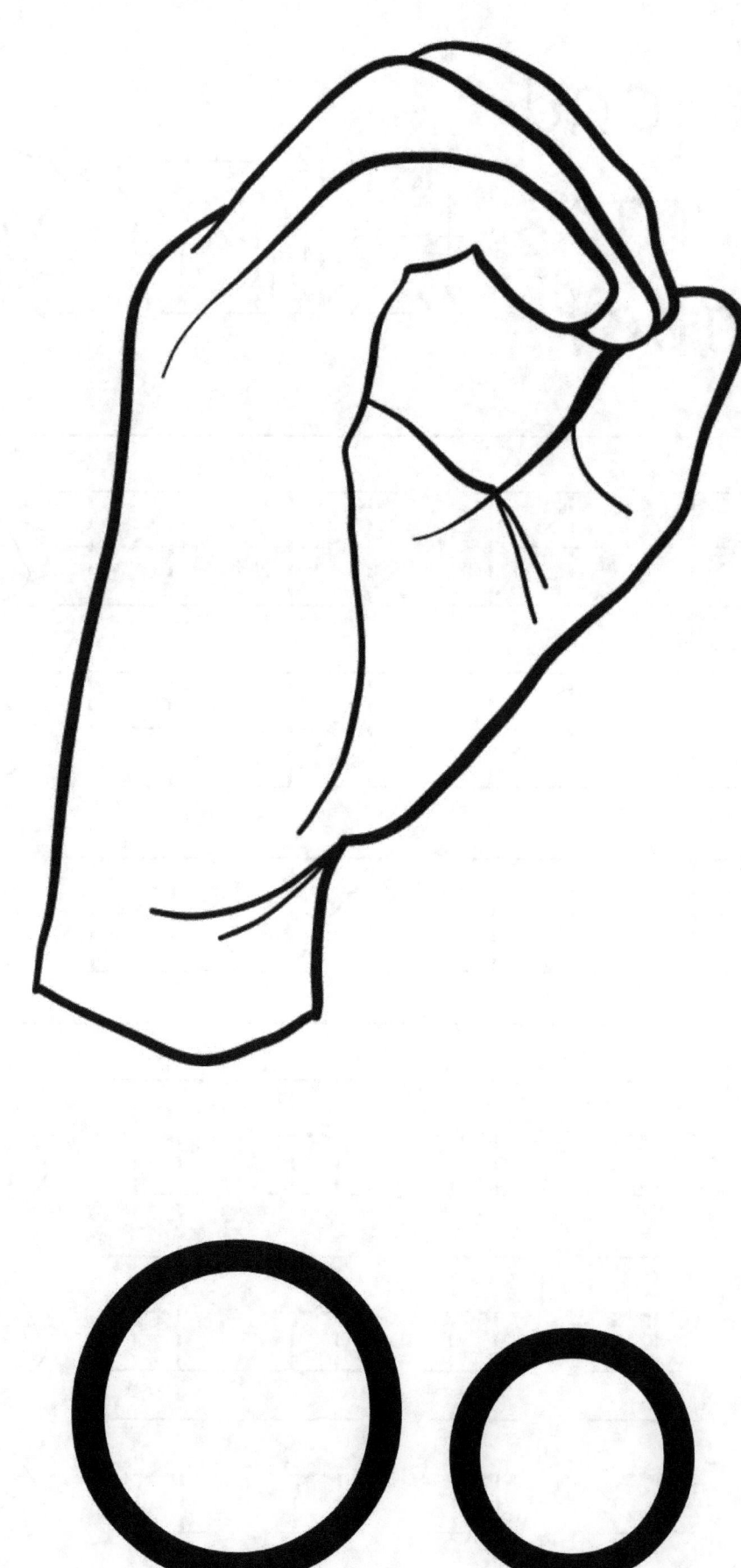

Oo

Trace and Sign the Alphabet

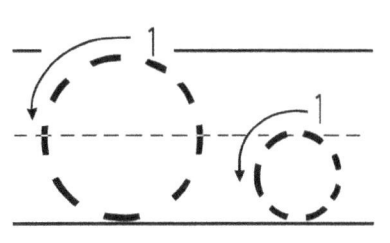

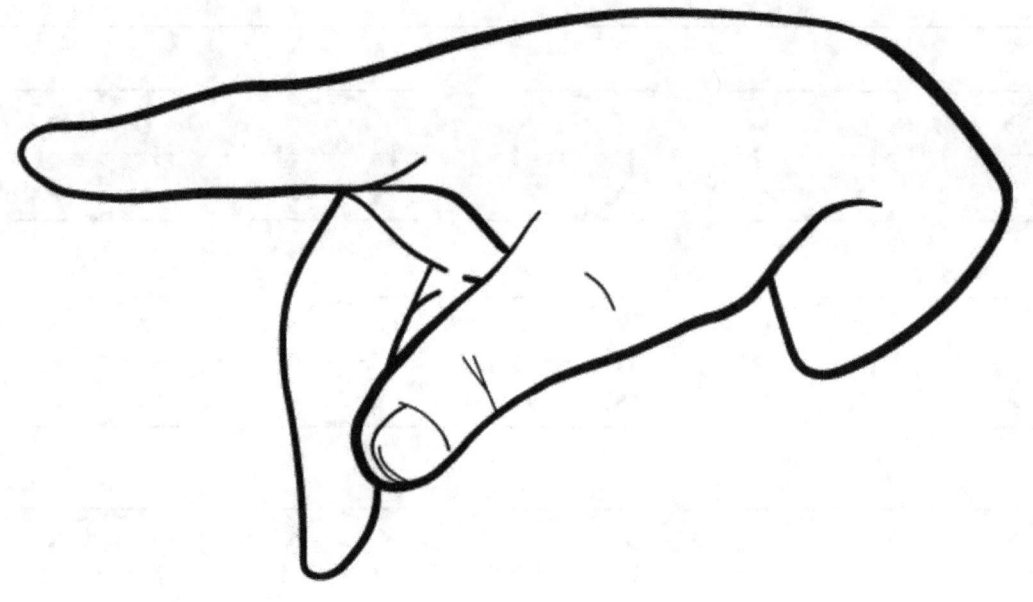

Pp

Trace and Sign the Alphabet

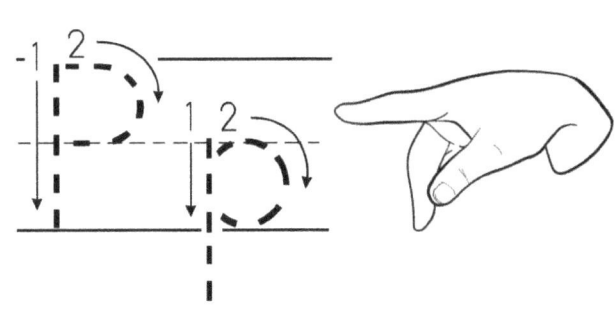

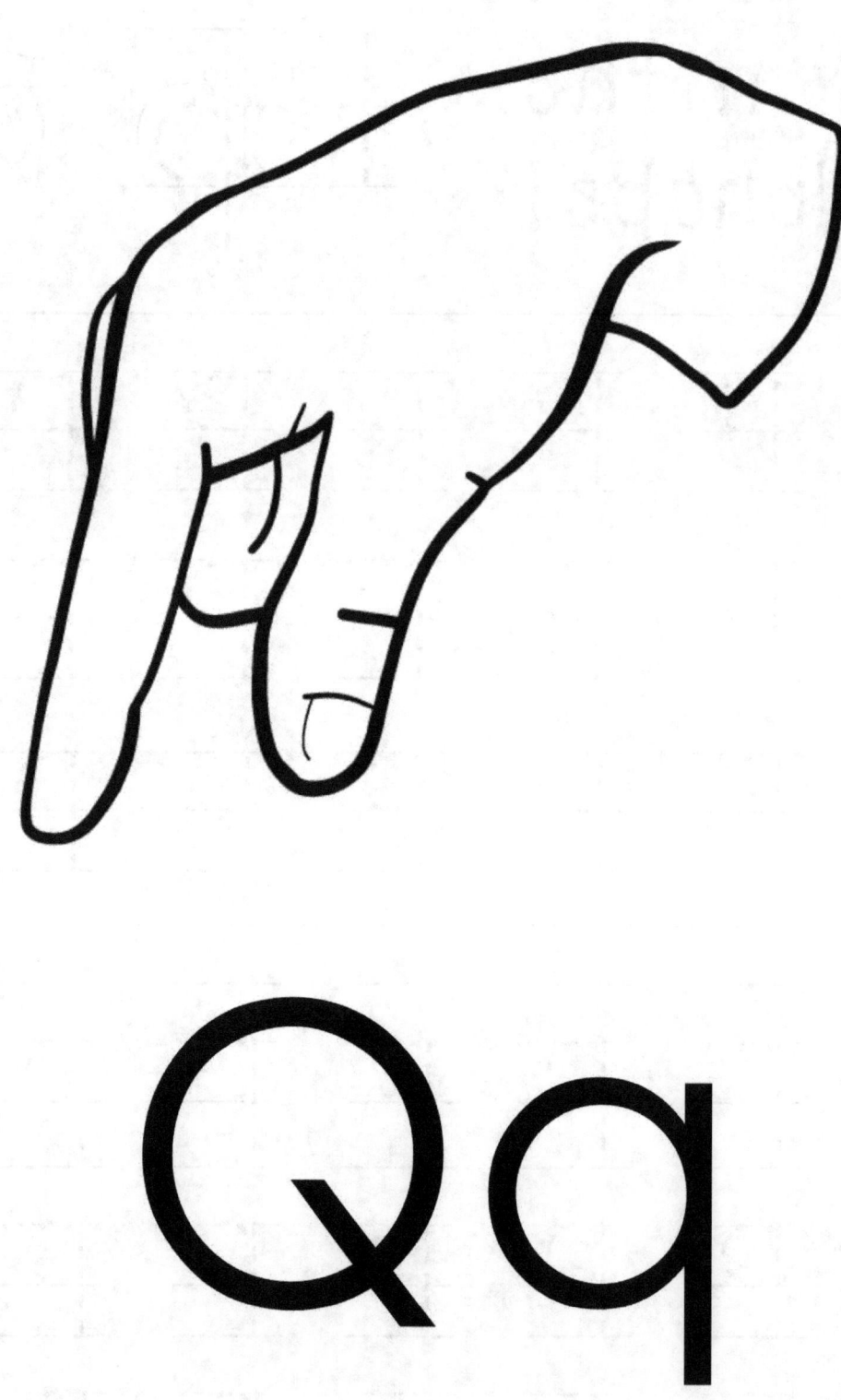

Qq

Trace and Sign the Alphabet

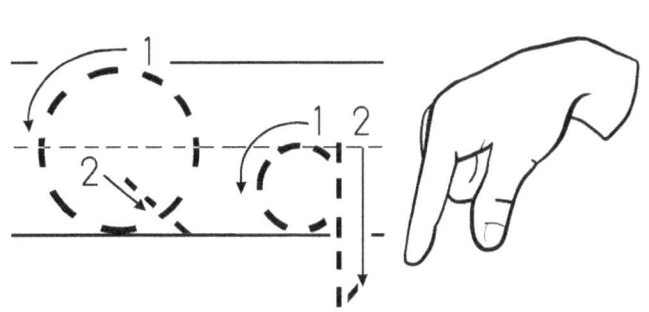

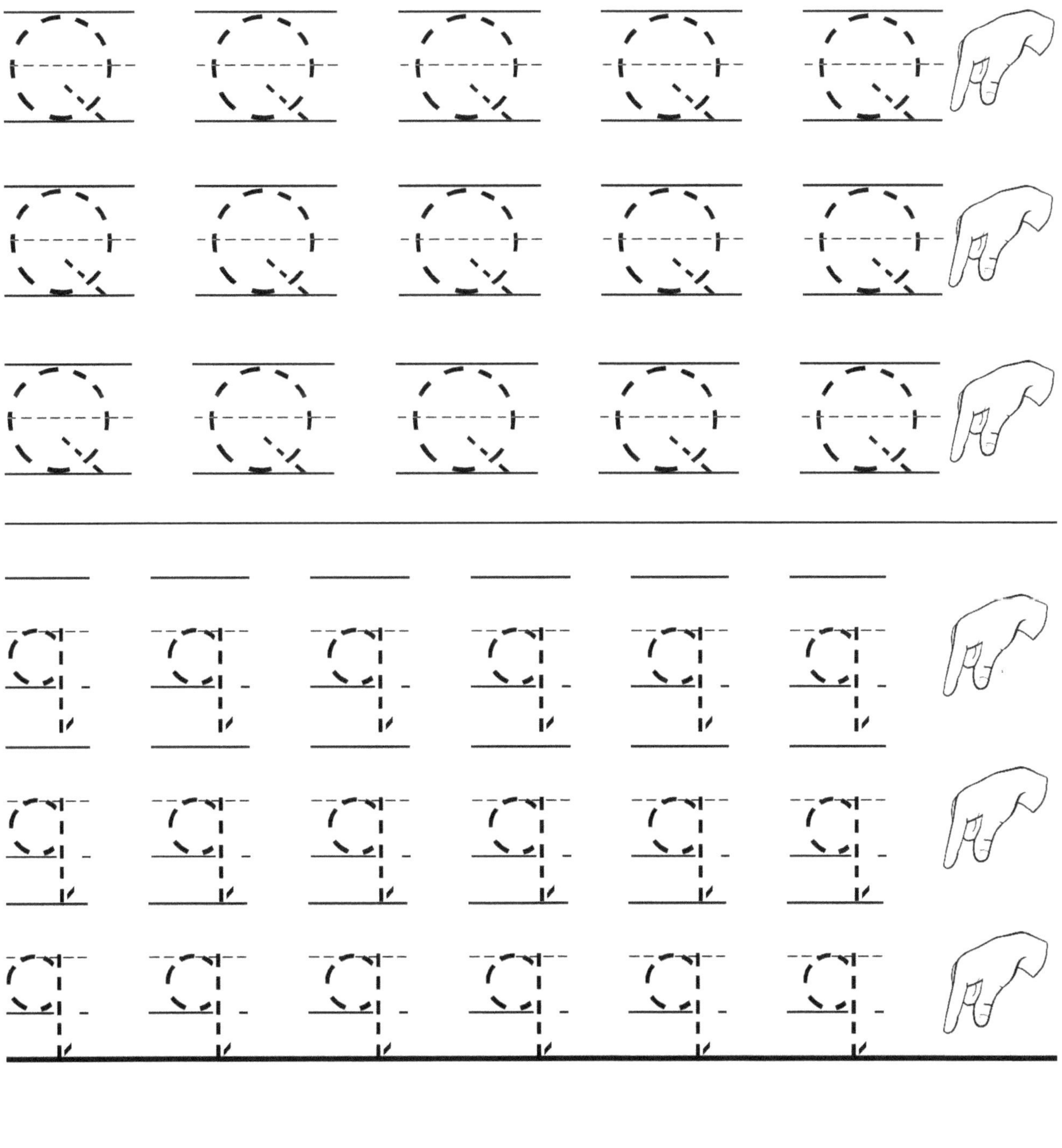

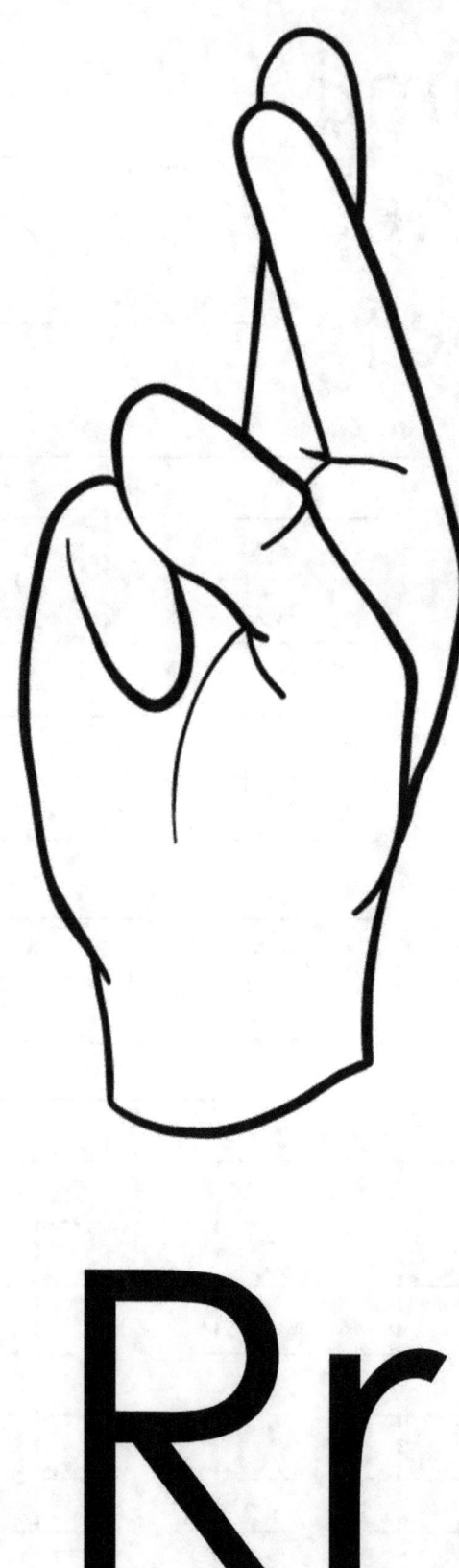

Rr

Trace and Sign the Alphabet

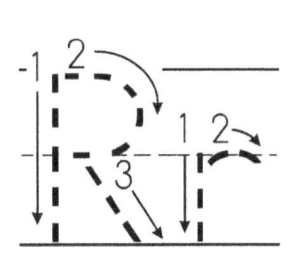

Ss

Trace and Sign the Alphabet

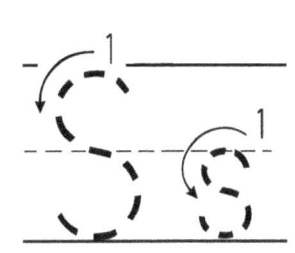 

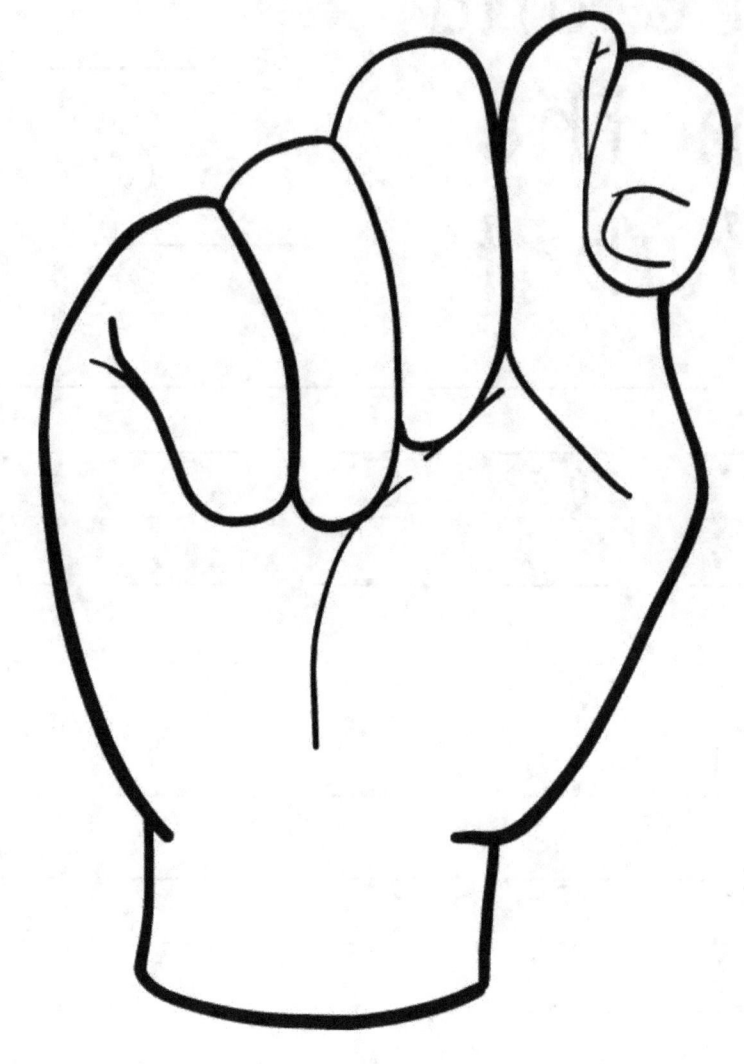

Tt

Trace and Sign the Alphabet

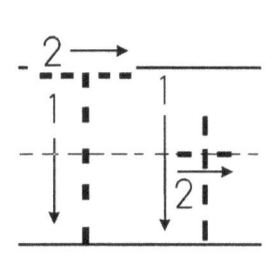

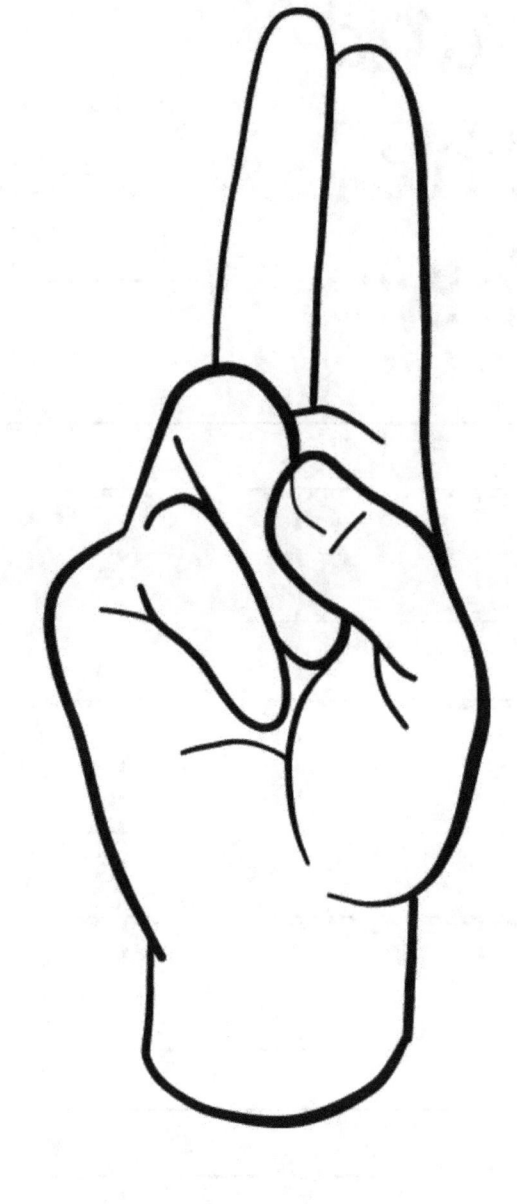

Uu

Trace and Sign the Alphabet

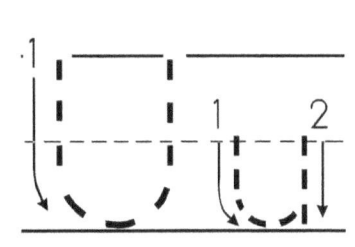 

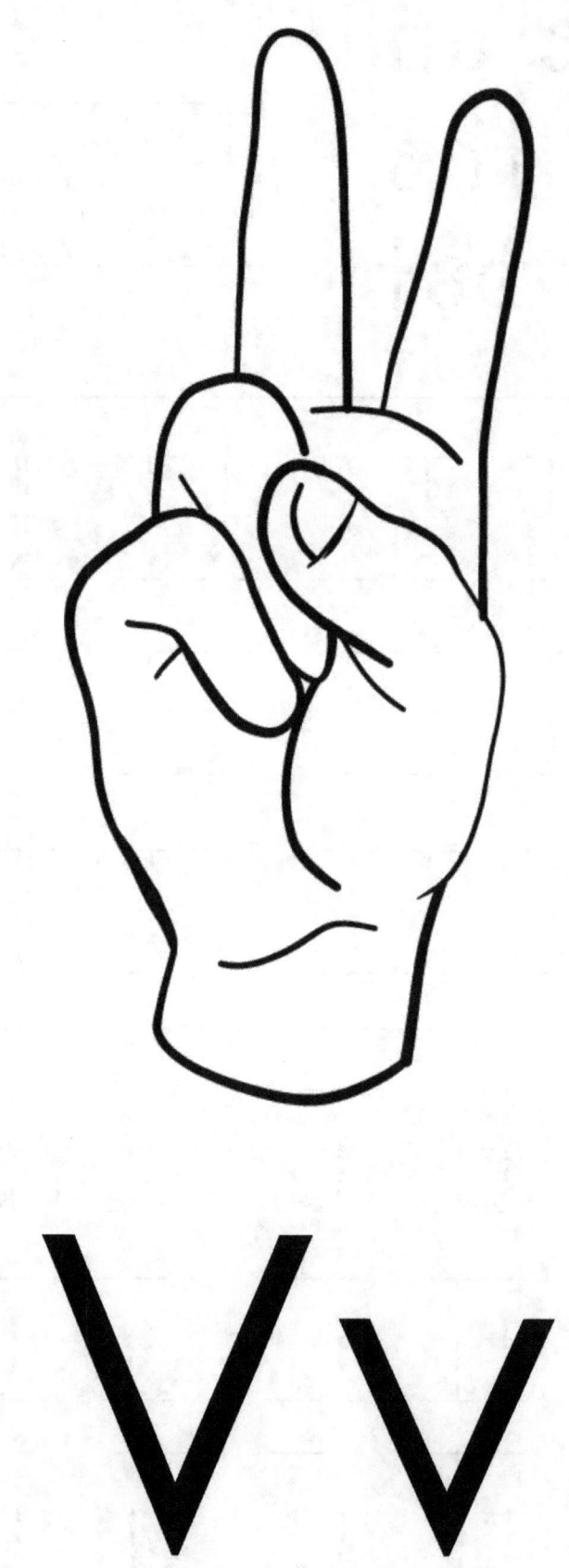

Vv

Trace and Sign the Alphabet

V V V V V

V V V V V

V V V V V

v v v v v v v

v v v v v v v

v v v v v v v

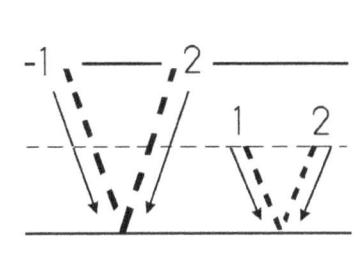

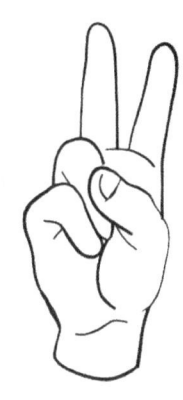

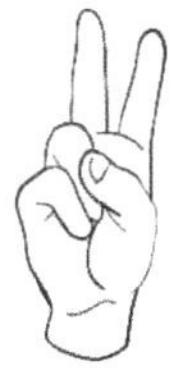

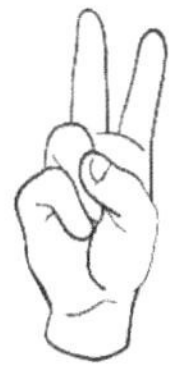

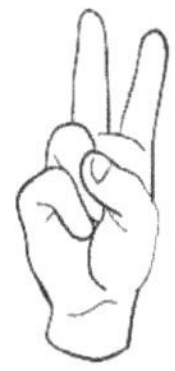

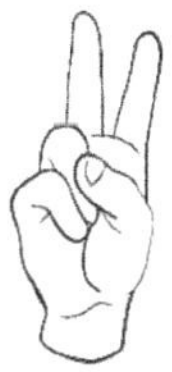

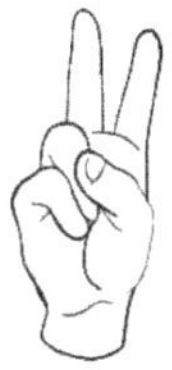

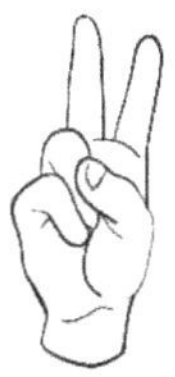

Ww

Trace and Sign the Alphabet

W W W W

W W W W

W W W W

w w w w w w

w w w w w w

w w w w w w

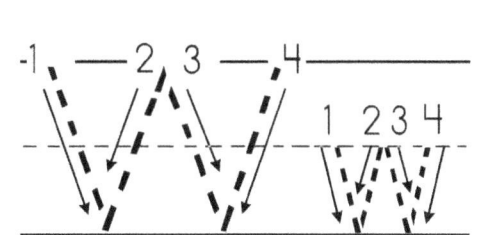

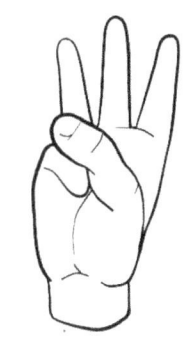

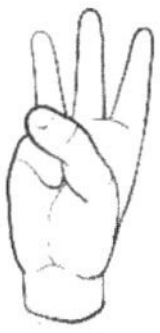

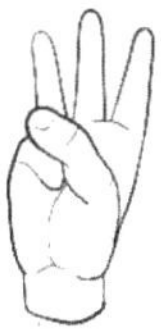

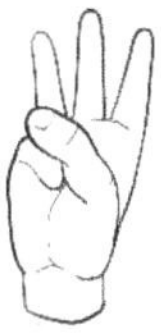

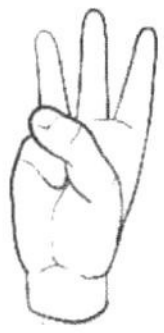

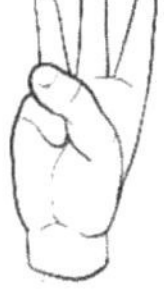

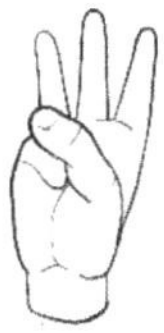

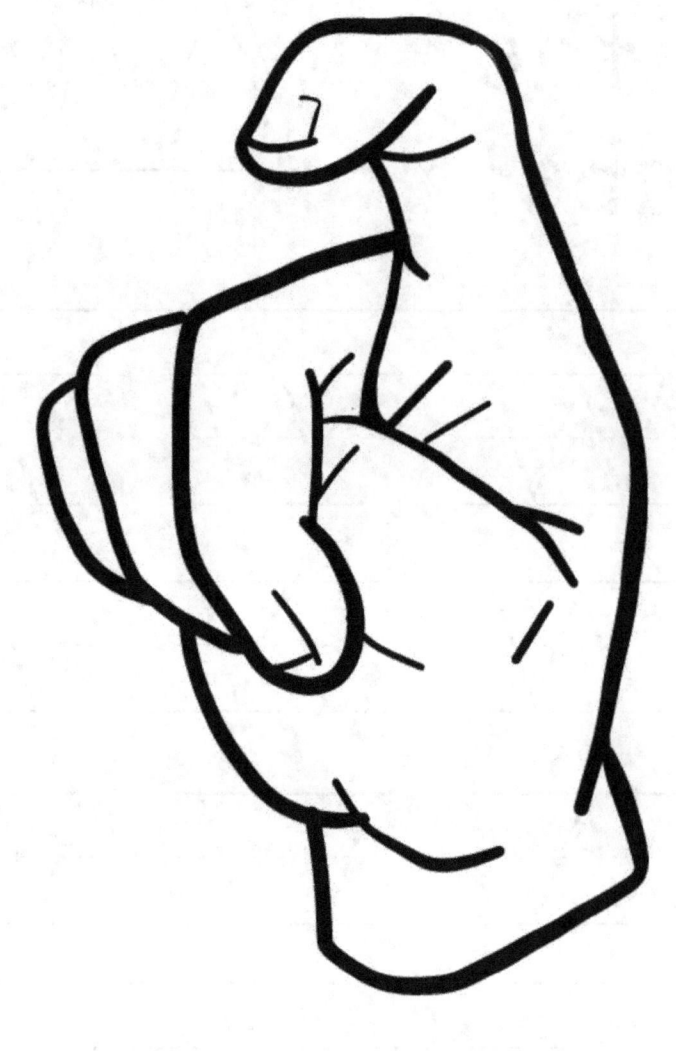

Xx

Trace and Sign the Alphabet

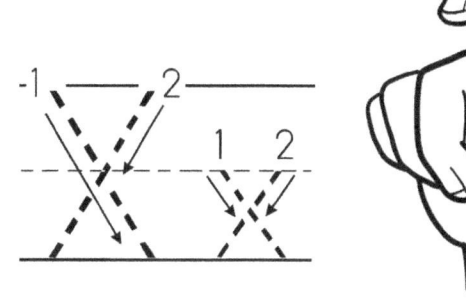

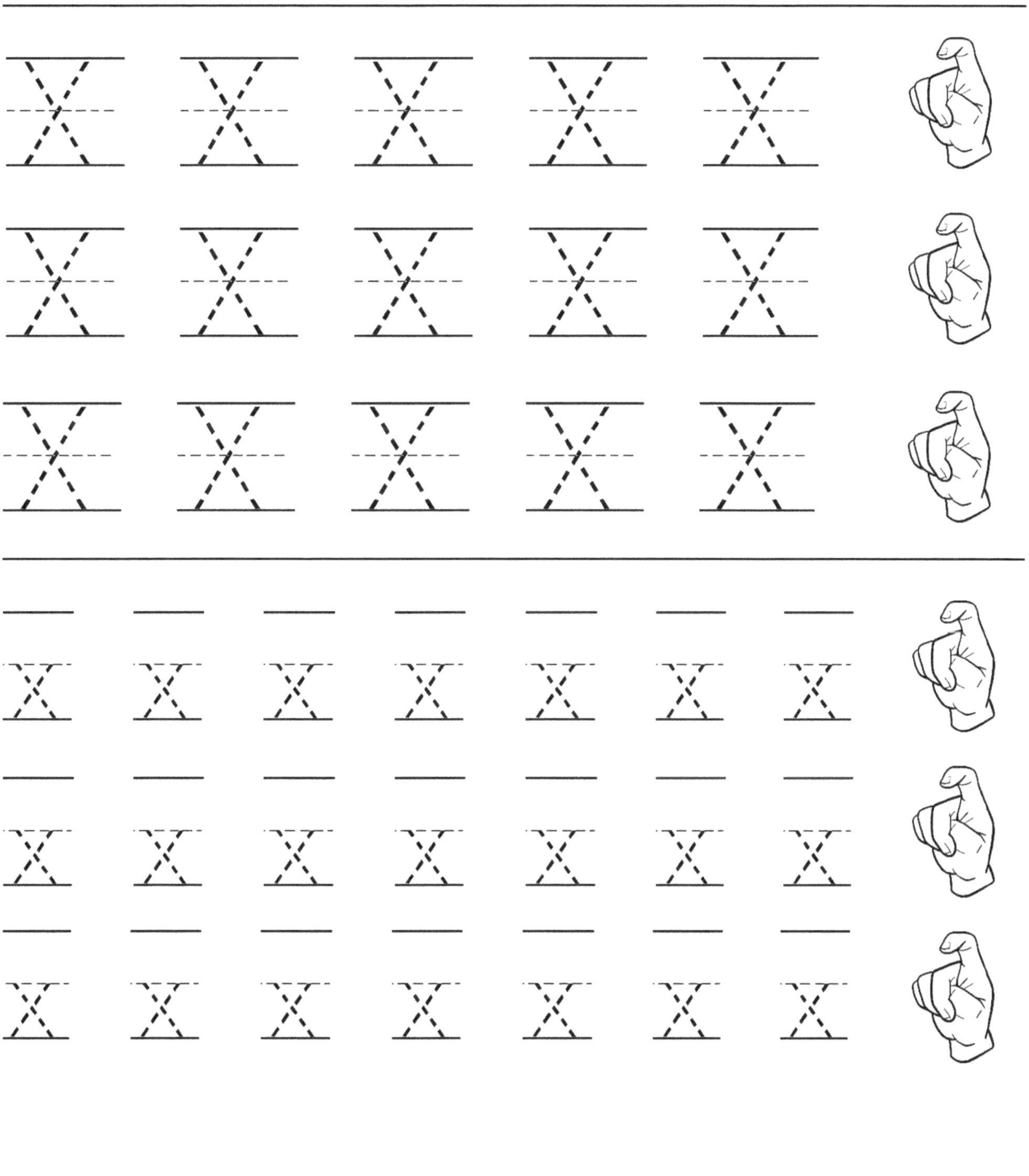

Yy

Trace and Sign the Alphabet

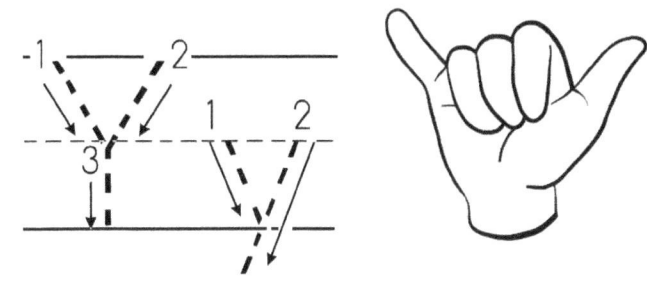

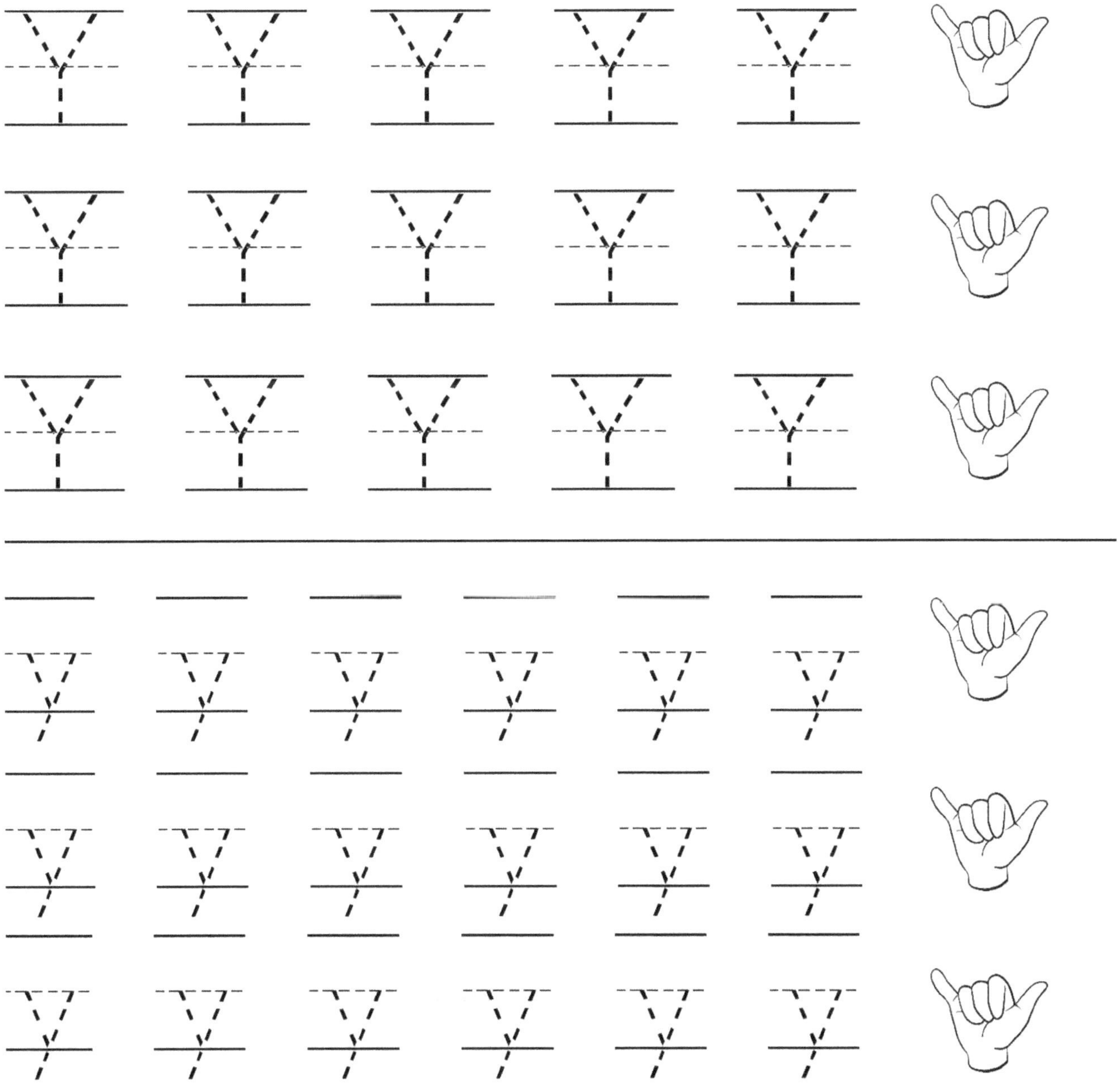

Z

Zz

Trace and Sign the Alphabet

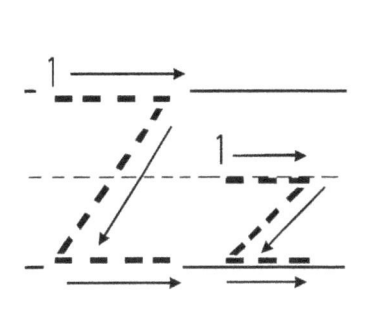

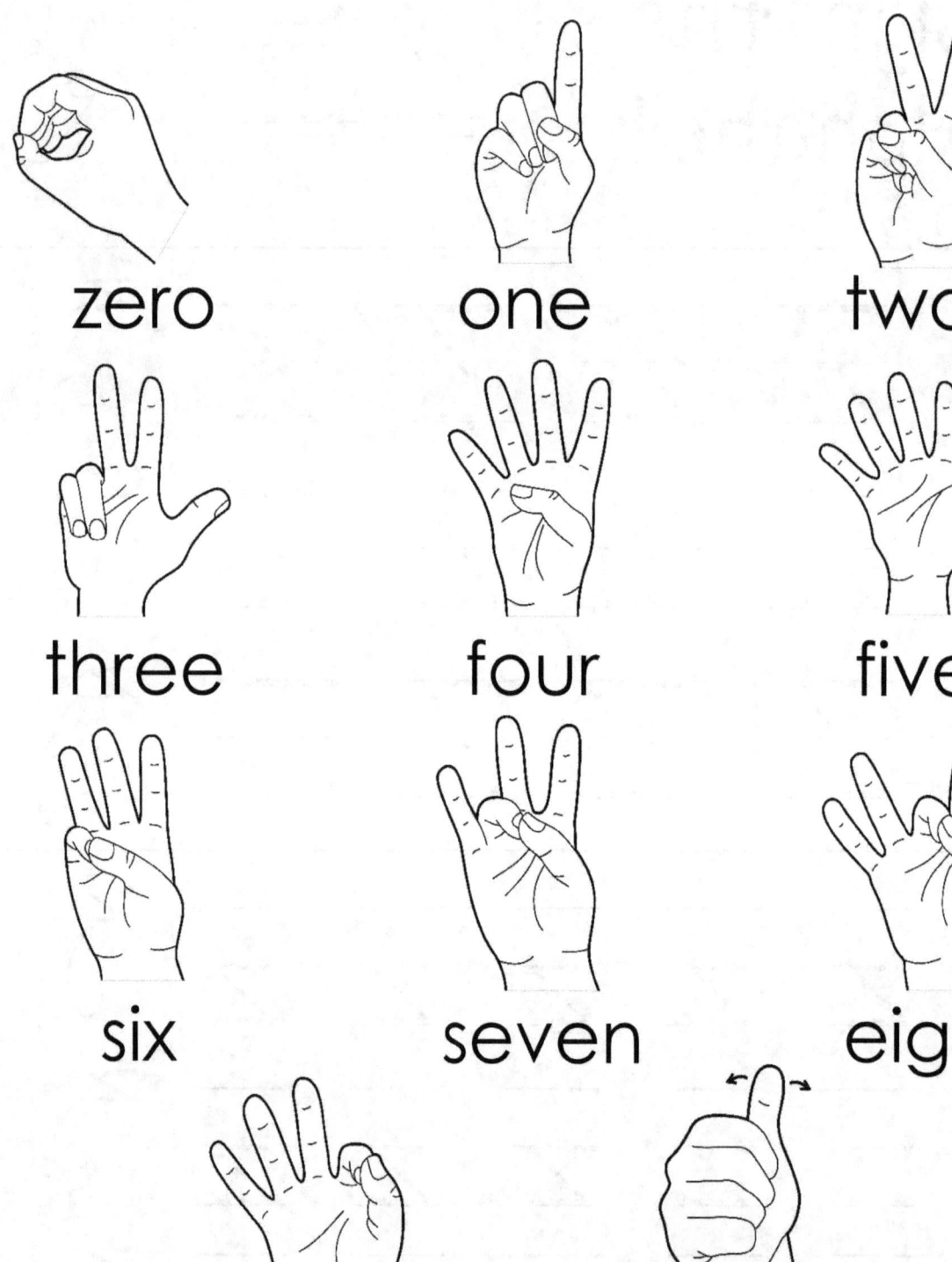

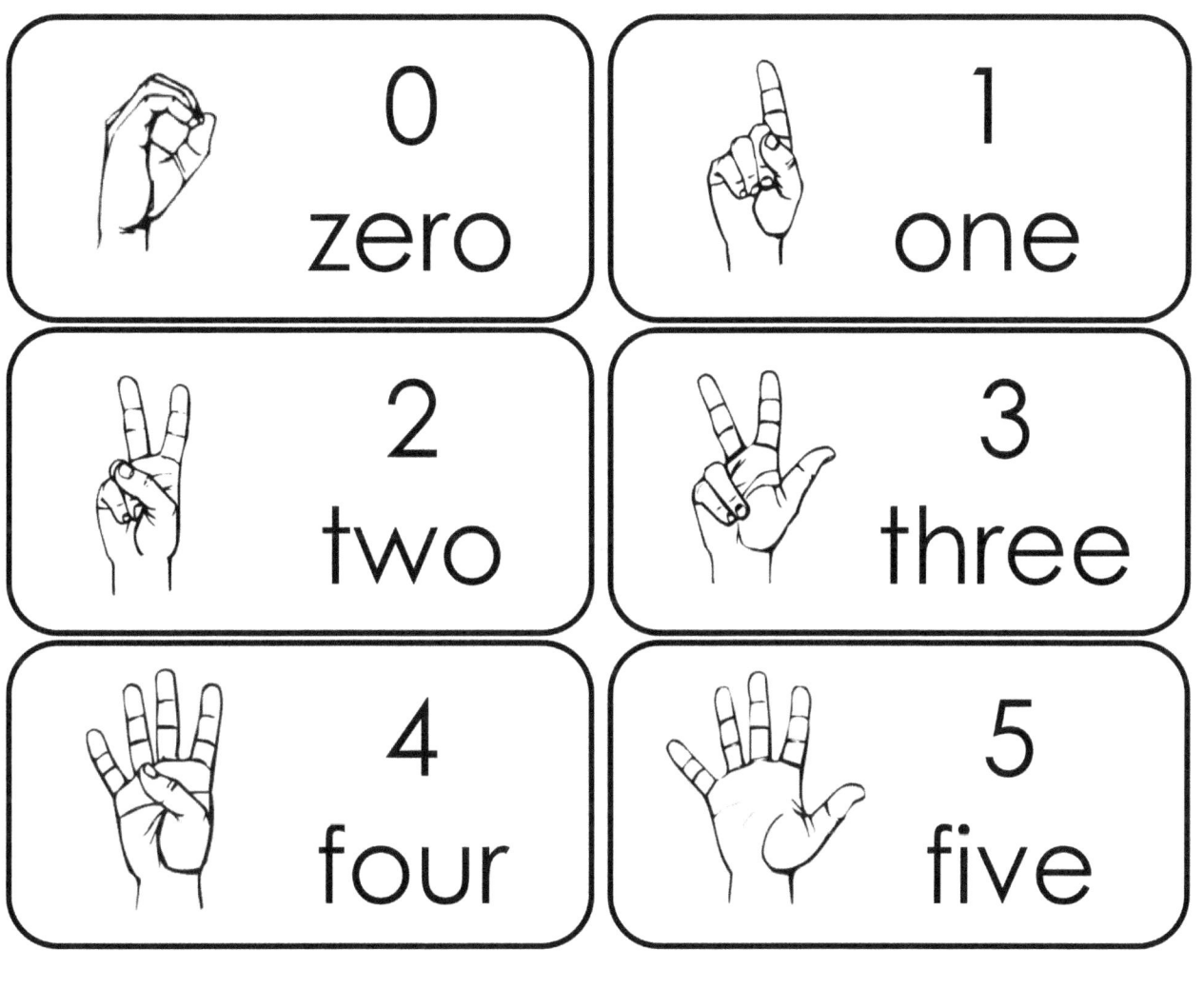

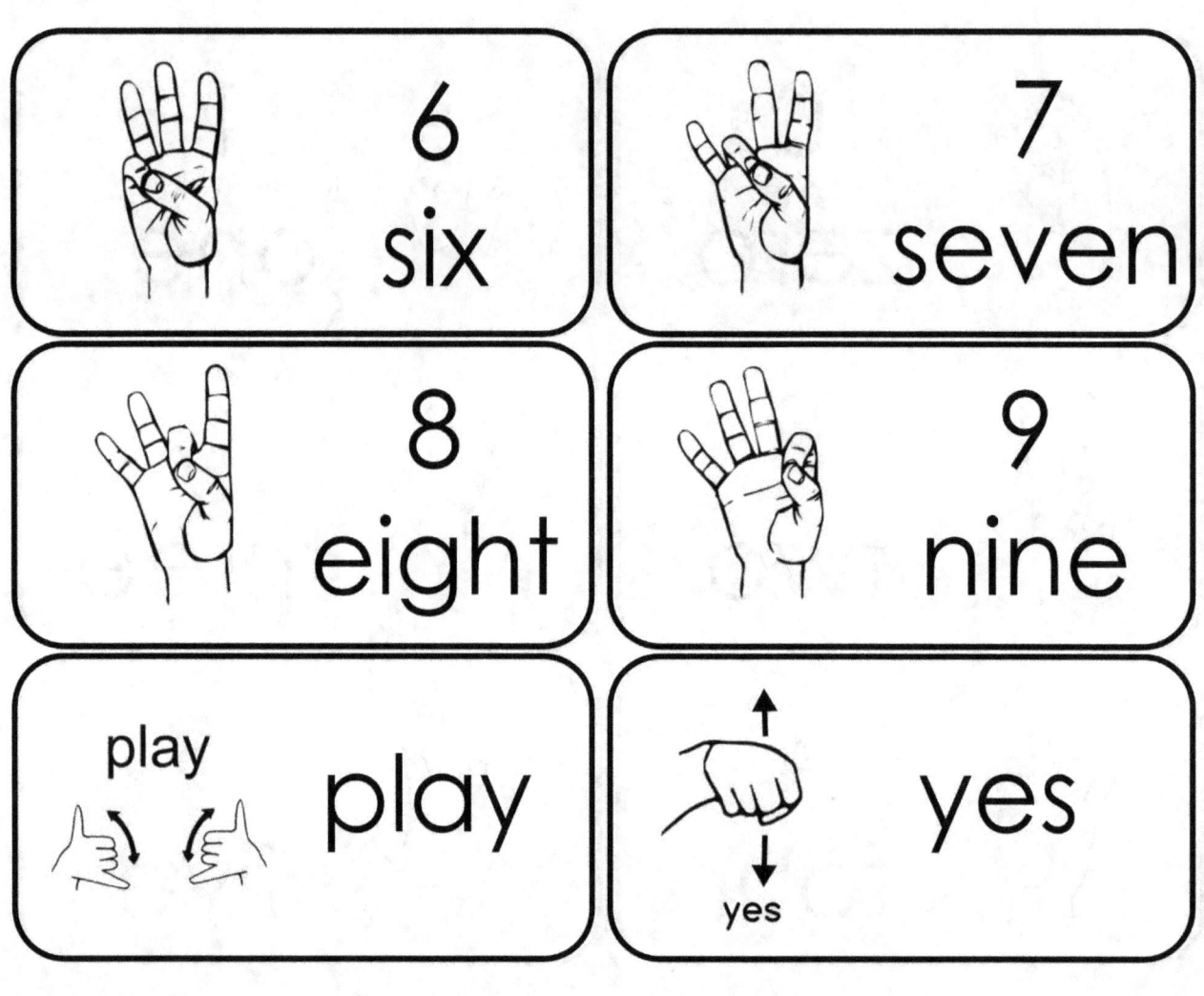

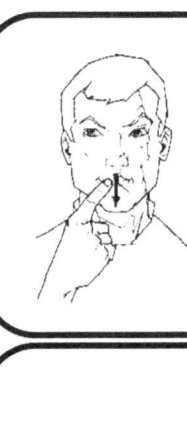 red

 orange

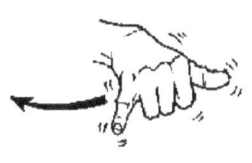 yellow

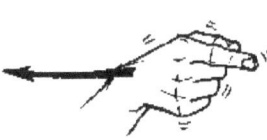 green

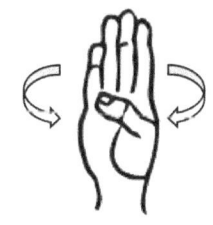 blue

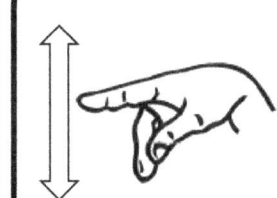 purple

 Brown

Thank You

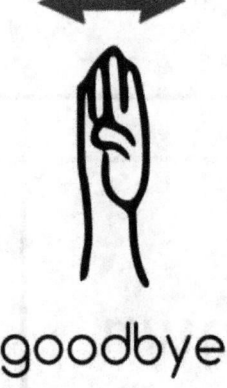

goodbye

goodbye